CREATURE CAMOUFLAGE

HIDING IN
FORESTS

Deborah Underwood

Raintree

www.raintreepublishers.co.uk
Visit our website to find out more information about Raintree books.

To order:
☎ Phone 0845 6044371
🖶 Fax +44 (0) 1865 312263
💻 Email myorders@raintreepublishers.co.uk

Customers from outside the UK please telephone +44 1865 312262

Raintree is an imprint of Capstone Global Library Limited, a company incorporated in England and Wales having its registered office at 7 Pilgrim Street, London, EC4V 6LB – Registered company number: 6695582

Text © Capstone Global Library Limited 2011
First published in hardback in 2011
First published in paperback in 2012
The moral rights of the proprietor have been asserted.

Edited by Rebecca Rissman and Nancy Dickmann
Designed by Joanna Hinton Malivoire
Picture research by Tracy Cummins
Originated by Capstone Global Library
Printed and bound in China by Leo Paper Products Ltd

ISBN 978 0 431 01132 5 (hardback)
15 14 13 12 11
10 9 8 7 6 5 4 3 2 1

ISBN 978 1 406 22001 8 (paperback)
16 15 14 13 12
10 9 8 7 6 5 4 3 2 1

British Library Cataloguing in Publication Data
Underwood, Deborah.
 Hiding in forests. -- (Creature camouflage)
 1. Forest animals--Juvenile literature. 2. Camouflage (Biology)--Juvenile literature.
 I. Title II. Series
 591.4'72'09152-dc22

Acknowledgements
We would like to thank the following for permission to reproduce photographs: Getty Images pp. 6 (David Tipling), 9 (altrendo nature), 11, 12 (Panoramic Images), 15, 16 (Ben Hall), 19, 20 (Gary Buss), 21, 22 (Mattias Klum); Minden Pictures pp. 17, 18 (Nature Production/Seiichi Meguro); naturepl.com pp. 23, 24 (© Staffan Widstrand), 25, 26 (© Rachel Hingley); Photolibrary pp. 13, 14 (Oxford Scientific (OSF); Shutterstock pp. 4 (© SNEHIT), 5 (© Alexandru Axon), 7 (© Brian Dunne), 8 (© Sascha Burkard), 10 (© Rusty Dodson), 27 (© Smirnof), 28 (© Ronnie Howard), 29 (© blind shot).

Cover photograph of a tawny owl (Strix aluco) in tree trunk reproduced with permission of naturepl.com (© David Tipling).

We would like to thank Michael Bright for his invaluable help in the preparation of this book.

Every effort has been made to contact copyright holders of any material reproduced in this book. Any omissions will be rectified in subsequent printings if notice is given to the publisher.

All the Internet addresses (URLs) given in this book were valid at the time of going to press. However, due to the dynamic nature of the Internet, some addresses may have changed, or sites may have changed or ceased to exist since publication. While the author and publisher regret any inconvenience this may cause readers, no responsibility for any such changes can be accepted by either the author or the publisher.

Contents

Some words are printed in bold, **like this**. You can find out what they mean by looking in the glossary.

What are forests like?

Forests are places where trees are the main type of plant. There are different types of forests. **Boreal forests** have trees with needle-shaped leaves.

Most trees with needle-shaped leaves do not change colour.

The trees in some forests have leaves that change colour.

The animals in this book live in **temperate forests**. These forests have four **seasons**. Most trees in temperate forests lose their leaves in the autumn.

Living in a forest

Many kinds of animals live in a forest. Some forest animals have special body **features** to help them **survive**. These features are called **adaptations**.

Woodpeckers use their strong beaks to dig nest holes in forest trees.

Black bears eat fruit, nuts, and honey. They also hunt other animals.

Some animals survive by eating other animals. These animals are called **predators**. The animals they eat are called **prey**.

What is camouflage?

Camouflage is an **adaptation** that helps animals hide. The colour of an animal's skin, fur, or feathers may match the things around it.

This squirrel's brown fur matches the tree.

A green luna moth on a tree looks like a leaf.

The shape of an animal may camouflage it, too. Some animals are shaped like sticks or leaves. Why do you think animals need to hide?

Some **predators** hide so they can creep up on **prey** animals. Prey animals hide so they won't become a predator's lunch!

This copperhead snake's brown colours help it hide in dead leaves.

Find the forest animals

Lynx

The lynx is a type of cat that lives in northern forests. Lynx hunt and eat other animals. Their fur colour helps them hide as they hunt.

CAMOUFLAGED

Lynx eat small animals, such as squirrels and birds. Some lynx also hunt bigger animals, such as deer. After they creep up on **prey**, they pounce!

REVEALED

Spotted owlet

Spotted owlets have feathers that **blend in** with tree **bark**. This **camouflage** helps to hide them from larger birds that might eat them.

Spotted owlets mainly hunt at night. An owl sits quietly on a tree branch. When a small animal passes below, the owl swoops down and grabs it!

REVEALED

Roe deer

Adult roe deer have reddish-brown coats in summer. Can you see how a deer's coat helps it hide in the forest? In winter, the deer grow grey or brown coats.

Young roe deer are called fawns. Their coats are brown with light spots. A fawn lies on the ground while its mother looks for food. The spots help the fawn **blend in** with the forest floor.

Siberian flying squirrel

Siberian flying squirrels have coats that change colour, too. They become silvery grey in winter. This makes it hard for **predators** to see them in the snow.

CAMOUFLAGED

Flying squirrels glide through the air. They have flaps of skin between their front and back legs. When the squirrels jump from trees, the skin flaps catch the wind.

REVEALED

Stick insects

If you want to hide in a tree, it helps to look like a stick! The shape and colour of a stick insect is a great **camouflage**.

When stick insects sense danger, they stay very still. This makes them look even more like real sticks.

REVEALED

Grey wolf

The colour of grey wolves' coats can help them hide as they hunt. Wolves live in groups called packs. A wolf pack hunts together.

The colour of wolves' coats depends partly on where they live. Wolves that live in snowy places may have whiter coats. This helps to **camouflage** them when they hunt in snow.

REVEALED

CAMOUFLAGED

Tawny frogmouth

The tawny frogmouth is a type of bird. It lives in parts of Australia. The bird's grey and brown feathers **blend in** with the trees. This helps to hide it from **predators**.

At night the tawny frogmouth hunts for insects, worms, and other food. During the day, the bird sits in a tree and stays very still. When it closes its eyes and points its head up, it looks like a broken branch!

REVEALED

CAMOUFLAGED

Peppered moth

A peppered moth on a tree trunk can be very hard to spot! Black and white wings help the moth hide from birds that want to eat it.

A female moth lays eggs. The eggs hatch into caterpillars. Peppered moth caterpillars are good at hiding, too. They look like twigs!

REVEALED

A hedgehog walks in some forest leaves.

If you visit a forest, look closely among the leaves and branches. You may see all sorts of animals hiding there!

Animals that stand out

Some forest animals don't hide. Their colours make them stand out. A male cardinal bird is a bright red colour. This helps him to attract a female.

A red male cardinal stands out in the green of the forest.

This ladybird's bright colour warns other animals not to eat it.

Ladybirds can make a nasty smell if other animals try to eat them. Their bright colour warns **predators** to stay away!

Glossary

adaptation special feature that helps an animal survive in its surroundings

bark tough, outer part of a tree trunk

blend in matches well with the things around it

boreal forest forest with long winters and trees with needle-shaped leaves, such as pine trees

camouflage adaptation that helps an animal blend in with the things around it

feature special part of an animal

predator animal that eats other animals

prey animal that other animals eat

seasons parts of the year that have different weather, such as spring, summer, autumn, and winter

survive stay alive

temperate forest forest that has four seasons

Find out more

Books to read

Animals: A Children's Encyclopedia
   (Dorling Kindersley, 2008)

Introducing Habitats: A Forest Habitat, Bobbie Kalman
   (Crabtree Publishing, 2006)

Saving Wildlife: Woodland and Forest Animals,
   Sonya Newland (Franklin Watts, 2010)

Websites

www.bbc.co.uk/nature/animals
Watch films and find out more about your favourite
animals on this BBC website.

www.nhm.ac.uk/kids-only/life/life-disguise
Visit the Natural Museum website to learn more about
animals that can disguise themselves.

Index